Contents

What Is Smooth?

These marbles are smooth. They have no cracks in them and no tiny bumps. The **surface** of a smooth thing is completely even.

SMOOTH AND ROUGH

Angela Royston

Heinemann Library
Chicago, Illinois

Designed by Jo Hinton-Malivoire and Tinstar Design Limited
Originated by Blenheim Colour, Ltd.
Printed and bound in China by South China Printing Company
Photo research by Maria Joannou and Sally Smith

07 06 05 04 03
10 9 8 7 6 5 4 3 2 1

Library of Congress Cataloging-in-Publication Data
    Royston, Angela.
   Smooth and rough / Angela Royston.
     c. cm. – (My world of science)
   Summary: A simple explanation of the physical properties of
smooth and rough objects, including examples of them in everyday life.
   Includes bibliographical references and index.
   ISBN 1-40340-859-9 (HC), 1-4034-3172-8 (Pbk)
   1. Surface roughness–Juvenile literature.   [1. Textures. 2. Surface roughness.]
I. Title. II. Series: Royston, Angela. My world of science.

TA418.7.R69 2003
620.1'1292–dc21

                                    2002009436

Acknowledgments
The author and publishers are grateful to the following for permission to reproduce copyright material:
pp. 4, 22 Chris Honeywell; pp. 5, 7, 10, 11, 12, 13, 14, 15, 17, 25, 26, 27, 28 Trevor Clifford; p. 6 Oxford Scientific Films; pp. 8, 18 PhotoDisc; p. 9 Raj Kamal/Robert Harding; pp. 16, 23 Pictor International; p. 19 Alamy Images; p. 20 Network Photographers; p. 21 Gareth Boden; p. 24 H. Rogers/Trip; p. 29 Robert Harding.

Cover photograph by Trevor Clifford.

Every effort has been made to contact copyright holders of any material reproduced in this book. Any omissions will be rectified in subsequent printings if notice is given to the publisher.

Some words are shown in bold, **like this.** You can find out what they mean by looking in the glossary.

You can tell if something is smooth by feeling it. If you run your fingers across the cover of this book, it will also feel smooth.

What Is Rough?

These stones are rough. Feel a rough stone with your fingers. You can feel the bumps, cracks, and dips in its **surface.**

These things feel rough. Some things are rougher than other things. The doormat is rougher than the school bag. The **bark** is the roughest thing here.

Naturally Smooth

Some things are naturally smooth. The leaves of an apple tree are not completely smooth. The skin of an apple feels smoother.

The insides of these shells are smoother than the outsides. Some of the pebbles are also smooth.

Smooth Cloth

Silk feels very smooth when you rub it on your skin. The ribbon in this girl's hair is almost as smooth as the silk scarf.

Bed sheets are smoother than **blankets.** Blankets keep you warm, but a smooth sheet feels more comfortable.

Smooth and Hard

Metals are very hard. They can also be very smooth. All of these things are made of smooth metals.

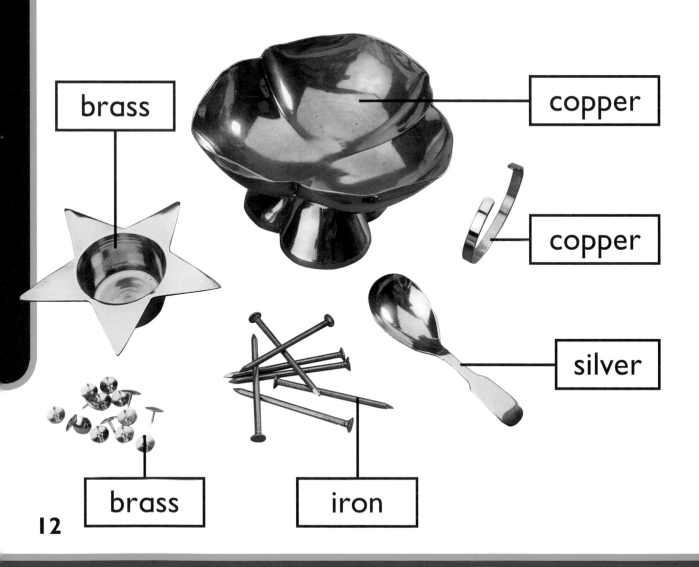

brass

copper

copper

silver

brass

iron

Other **materials** are smooth, too. The box is made of smooth plastic. The bottle is glass, and the cup is made of china.

Easy to Clean

Smooth things are easier to clean than rough things. Sinks, pans, and plates are all smooth. It is easy to wash them.

A pan scrubber is rougher than a sponge. The rough scrubber is better for rubbing away food that is stuck in a bowl.

Making Something Smooth

When two rough **surfaces** rub together, they become smoother. This wall has a rough patch. Rubbing it with sandpaper will make it smoother.

These shiny pebbles have been tumbled in a special machine. As they tumbled, they rubbed against each other. This made them smooth and **polished.**

Slipping and Sliding

Smooth **surfaces** can be slippery. Ice is smooth and very slippery. It is hard to stay on your feet when you are skating on ice.

This child is sliding down a metal slide. Metal is not as slippery as ice, but it is more slippery than wood.

Wet Surfaces

Water makes **surfaces** smooth. Wet surfaces are more slippery than dry ones. You must be careful not to slip on wet floors.

Do not run around the edge of a swimming pool. It is often wet and slippery. These children need to walk carefully.

Treads

These shoes have a deep **tread** cut into the soles. The tread makes the sole rough. Treads stop your shoes from slipping on smooth ground.

Rubber tires have treads cut into them, too. The treads help the wheels grip the ground. Mountain bikes have deep treads that grip slippery **surfaces.**

Friction

When two rough **surfaces** rub against each other, they stick together a little. This is called **friction.** Friction keeps things from sliding.

Push a box along the floor. When you let go, it slows down and stops. Friction between the box and the floor slows the box down.

Testing Surfaces

This boy is testing different **surfaces.** He is pushing a car on a wooden floor. The car rolls very far. The smooth wood makes little **friction.**

Rough surfaces make more friction than smooth surfaces. On this rough carpet, the car does not roll very far.

Using Rough Surfaces

These table mats are made of **raffia.**
Raffia is rough, so the mats are
bumpy. Plates will not slip off of
them easily.

These pages have rough bumps. This is a kind of writing called **Braille.** People who are blind feel the dots to read the words.

Glossary

bark outer layer of a tree's trunk

blanket warm bed cover made of wool or similar material

Braille writing that uses dots to make words

friction force that keeps two surfaces from sliding easily across each other

material what a thing is made of

polish rub a surface with something until it is shiny

raffia material made from the leaves of palm trees. It is used to make hats, mats, and baskets.

silk fine thread made by silk moth caterpillars. Silk thread is woven into cloth.

surface outside part of something

tread deep grooves and ridges cut into a rubber or plastic surface

tire rubber part of a bicycle or car wheel

More Books to Read

Llewellyn, Claire. *Plastic.* Danbury, Conn.: Scholastic Library Publishing, 2002

Marshall, John. *Go and Stop.* Vero Beach, Fla.: Rourke Publishing, LLC, 1995.

Mitchell, Melanie. *Metal.* Minneapolis: Lerner Publishing Group, 2002.

Index